Seeking the Lost: Sheep

Daniel Cramton

WestBow Press books may be ordered through booksellers or by contacting:

WestBow Press
A Division of Thomas Nelson & Zondervan
1663 Liberty Drive
Bloomington, IN 47403
www.westbowpress.com
844-714-3454

Because of the dynamic nature of the Internet, any web addresses or links contained in this book may have changed since publication and may no longer be valid. The views expressed in this work are solely those of the author and do not necessarily reflect the views of the publisher, and the publisher hereby disclaims any responsibility for them.

Scripture quotation taken from the Holy Bible, NEW INTERNATIONAL VERSION®, NIV® Copyright © 1973, 1978, 1984, 2011 by Biblica, Inc.® Used by permission. All rights reserved worldwide.

Line Artist: Onofrio Orlando with WMart Studio, Malta
Color Artist: Mariya Stoyanova, United Kingdom

www.remnantreaders.com

ISBN: 979-8-3850-3741-4 (sc)
ISBN: 979-8-3850-3742-1 (hc)
ISBN: 979-8-3850-3740-7 (e)

Library of Congress Control Number: 2024922885

Print information available on the last page.

WestBow Press rev. date: 01/29/2025

WESTBOW
PRESS®
A DIVISION OF THOMAS NELSON
& ZONDERVAN

Preface

Our God is an amazing God, and all glory belongs to Him for the stories shared. Because the work is for the glory of God, I want to make every book epic for Christ. I love the stories. I cherish the writing, and children love pictures with vibrant colors! I knew that in a world of increasing digital usage, these books must be special. They certainly are to me. At every stage and with every person, I have prayed over the project. Working on the children's books has allowed me to do something not just for God but with God. We hang out together as I write. Words will just flow as I think about the Biblical story, and then at some point I will come to a writer's block—a time when nothing seems to fit. There's a transition that I don't like or the direction of the story seems to be missing something. At that point, I pray again and then wait on Him to teach me what I don't know yet. Sometimes that waiting period is a few moments, sometimes days, sometimes weeks, but eventually the aha moment comes, and I know exactly what to do, and the writing process begins again. Then God gives me a mental image of how the pictures should look, which I relay to the artists. Several pages have brought tears to my eyes because of how they captured the exact intent, and I know God is working. There are many stories in the works for future books, and my hope is to have an assembly line of continuous releases. Funding is the only thing slowing us down. So, it's with my sincerest gratitude that I thank you for purchasing this book, allowing more work to be done for Christ. Only in eternity will we know the impact we have made. Thank you.

www.remnantreaders.com

There are many stories Jesus told.
They have lots of truths to behold.

Meant for light, not to condemn,

Adapted from Jesus's parables found in Luke 15.

HOLY BIBLE

Parables are what we call them.

These truths are worth more than gold,
So, listen carefully as they unfold.

By the Holy Spirit, you will see
These stories are about you and me.

For God wants to save everyone.

That's why He sent His only Son—

To show the world God's character
And how He deals with a sinner.

The truth revealed will bring you to tears,
Give you hope, and drive away your fears.

So take to heart the messages they bear.
Learn them well so you, too, can share—

This love and grace, and mercy too,
The sweet salvation for me and you.

Lost Sheep

Lost Coin

Lost Son

Now let us begin a story of three,
And ask yourself, *Which one is me?*

The first is about a sheep gone missing.
The Shepherd led, but it wasn't listening.

As the Shepherd's voice got farther away,
The sheep is distracted and went astray.

Running and playing and eating its food,
It's totally clueless until a cow mooed.

Startled and scared, it looks up and around,
But no sheep or Shepherd could be found.

The sheep is in the wilderness and all alone.
Where, oh where, is the Shepherd's tone?

It never intended to get so distracted.
Now there's consequences to the way it acted.

Fear and doubt welled up inside.
Now it looks for a place to hide.

It wandered away from the Shepherd's care
And now got caught in the devil's snare.

Trembling and shaking, it's a panic attack.

It knows it's lost but not how to get back.

Is this the end for the poor little fellow?
He starts to cry and lets out a bellow.

Back to the Shepherd, who's counting His sheep.
"Ninety-eight, ninety-nine ..." He jumps up with a leap.

"One has gone missing; it's not with the rest!

Apart from Me, how can it be blessed?"

What will He do? There's no need to guess.
He leaves the ninety-nine in the wilderness.

The Shepherd takes off in a sprinting run,
Out in search for the lost little one.

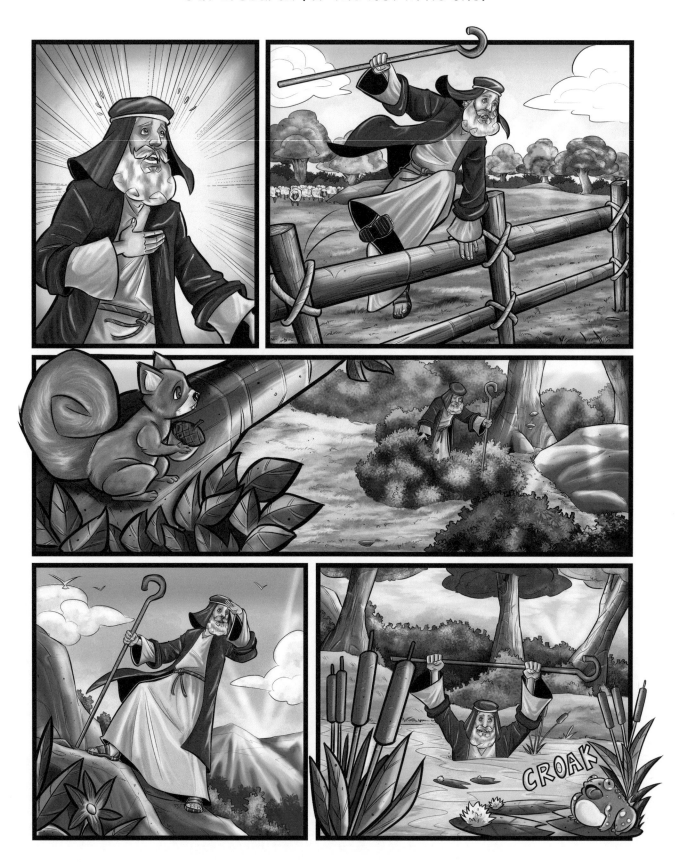

Around the bushes and through the trees,
Over the mountains and down valleys.

The Shepherd is calling, in a voice so clear
For the one lost sheep He deems so dear.

The character of the Shepherd is so kind.

All this effort for one lost sheep to find.

On the lookout for the one that is lost,
The Shepherd will find it no matter the cost.

There it is! The Shepherd can see.
Now He sets, the little one free!

It feels guilt and shame for how it behaved,
But the Shepherd smiles, "Now you are saved!"

Then He sings a song to rejoice,
And the sheep is delighted to hear His voice.

On His shoulder, the sheep is laid.
It does not matter that it disobeyed.

This little one, so precious to Him,
Is why He risked life and limb.

The Shepherd returns. He carried His sheep
Back to the fold and into His keep.

He calls to all His neighbors and friends
For a party invitation that He extends.

"I lost my sheep, but now it's found.
Let's have the biggest party around."

Joy is in heaven over one sinner to repent,
More than the other 99 percent.

This is the story of the lost little sheep.

Salvation is free, but it didn't come cheap.

That concludes the first parable.
It's a happy ending, and that's incredible.

It has cost about $21,600 to bring *Seeking the Lost: Sheep* into your hands. It was written in 2020. Thank you again for purchasing the book, as the proceeds propel future releases on a faster timeline. Donations are also welcomed and appreciated to further the Lord's work.

The Lord bless you and keep you; the Lord make His face shine on you and be gracious to you; the Lord turn His face toward you and give you peace.
—Numbers 6:24-26 (NIV)

www.remnantreaders.com

Author's Note

Each book goes through seven stages:
1. Biblical concept idea
2. Written poetry
3. Conceptual sketches
4. Line art drawing
5. Photoshop color art
6. Editing
7. Publishing

Books currently in the works include:

Seeking the Lost: Coin (stage 5, now being colored)

Seeking the Lost: Son (stage 4, drawn and awaiting color)

A Wise Warning (stage 4, drawn and awaiting color)

Wonderful Wages (stage 3, written and starting conceptual sketches)

Scattered Seeds (stage 3, written and starting conceptual sketches)

Gone Fishin' (stage 2, being written)

Printed in the United States
by Baker & Taylor Publisher Services